The Sensible Scripture Study

The Sensible Scripture Study

Steve Kellmeyer

Bridegroom Press   Plano, TX

Scripture quotations taken from the Douay-Rheims translation.

Copyright 2007 by Steven Kellmeyer
ISBN: 1-60104-003-2
ISBN-13: 978-1-60104-003-9

Printed in the U.S.A.

Bridegroom Press
2901 Country Place Dr., Plano, TX 75075
www.bridegroompress.com
E-mail: info@bridegroompress.com
Phone : 972-758-9209

Contents

Proverbs 1:1-6 provides additional confirmation. In this passage, Solomon, the wisest Old Testament man who ever lived, tells us that he is writing the book of Proverbs in order to teach us how to understand a proverb. That is, he will use proverbs to explain proverbs. Jesus was a wiser man than Solomon (Mt 12:42), and for a period of nearly 200 years before and after the Incarnation, He was the only rabbi who taught using parables (Mt 13:34-35). Jesus used parables to explain the parable of salvation history. In fact, the whole of Scripture is a parable which explains that one Parable.

Yet, even though Jesus spoke constantly in parable and figure — indeed, even the famous John 3:16 is immediately preceded by a typological analogy to the serpent that Moses lifted up in the desert — Scripture witnesses again and again how He continually had to explain every figure He used (e.g. Jn 10:6). This is important for two reasons. First, it confirms what both Luke and Matthew were inspired to record about Jesus: "the people who sat in darkness have seen a great light" (Mt 4:14-16, Lk 1:78-79). Nearly all the people who lived under the Old Testament were incapable of reading Scripture with the necessary understanding. Their minds needed to be enlightened to understand the parable they and their ancestors daily lived out. Second, as Mt 13:10 records, Jesus gave the apostles a gift which none but the prophets who lived under the Old Testament had ever received - He gave them the ability to understand what the Old Testament "parables" pointed to.

Indeed, Jesus promises exactly that in John 16:25 — there would come a time when He would speak to them plainly and not in any figure. However, He makes this promise just scant hours before His own death, just minutes before the Twelve break and run like water. When is the promise fulfilled? Only after the Resurrection: "Then he opened their minds to understand the scriptures." (Luke 24:45).

It is in the period between the Resurrection and the Ascension that Jesus teaches the Apostles how to read Scripture typologically, a skill which no one besides the prophets ever possessed. Even after His Resurrection, this skill was a uniquely apostolic gift. Thus, the Thessalonicans in Acts 17 who rejected apostolic guidance in how to read Scriptures continued on in darkness, while the Bereans, who desired the full understanding of Scripture, were unable to attain it without the guidance first of Paul and then of Silas and Timothy, whom Paul left behind to continue in their instruction. The extent to which this apostolic guidance is necessary is underscored by Scripture itself. No person or group of people in Scripture attained an accurate understanding of who Jesus was or what He did without apostolicly authorized guidance, despite the fact that knowledge of Jesus was widespread: "this thing was not done in a corner" (Acts 26:26).

This apostolic gift explains why the epistles are rich in the fourfold sense of Scripture. The whole letter to the Hebrews, especially passages like 8:4-5; 9:24; and 10:1, refer again and again to the Old Testament through the four-fold sense. Col 2:16-17; Gal 4:24-30; 2 Pet 2:6; James 5:10; and Jude 7 all demonstrate the concept, while 1 Cor 10:1-11 shows the principle at its clearest. Paul talks of the Israelites being "baptized into Moses" when they crossed the Red Sea, yet Exodus never speaks of this. Similarly, Exodus does not describe any food or drink as "supernatural," nor does it describe a rock which followed the Israelites. Paul is seeing the Old Testament in a new way, a way to which he was blind prior to being knocked off his horse. This is why he lists several of the excesses of the Israelites and remarks, "Now these things happened to them as a warning, but they were written down for our instruction, upon whom the end of the ages has come."

The Old Testament is written for our instruction — it is a morality play in which every event both really happened and simultaneously points beyond itself to eternity. Peter, Paul, James, Jude — each was inspired by God to demonstrate this new clarity of vision. Through the epistles, God shows us that the four-fold sense of Scripture is necessary for an accurate understanding of New Testament events — indeed, even simple references to Jesus like "Lamb of God," "the Good Shepherd," and "the Paschal Victim" are nonsensical outside of the four-fold sense.

The Apostles, through the assistance of the Holy Spirit, were inspired to begin unlocking the Scriptures which had lain hidden in plain sight for so long. This process of unlocking Scripture continued throughout the early Church. The great Christians of the first millennium knew the technique intimately and wielded it like a two-edged sword against heretical opponents. They saw the Apostolic reading of Old Testament Scripture as the beginning of a process which they were supposed to bring to fruition. They knew this method to be the divinely inspired method.

This is why we never see Jesus or the Apostles whipping out a dictionary to check the gender of a noun or the aorist tense of a verb. Paul never diagrams a sentence. The task begun by Jesus and the Apostles is not yet complete — indeed, it may never be complete. It is still necessary for us today to search out the four-fold sense of Scripture in order to grasp the fullness of the divinely intended meaning in the Old and New Testaments.

How to Find the Four Senses

The art of reading according to the four senses has a few basic rules, but it is mostly an exercise in a kind of free association or poetry. The rules laid out are not formally listed anywhere in the Magisterium. Rather, they are derived from a study of how the Fathers of the Church went about their work. The basic conditions described below are meant to give you direction in your study.

The Primary Interpretive Principle: Why God Took Flesh

(1) God took flesh in order to establish the Church and her sacraments, through which all men are saved.

(2) He returns in the flesh — both in the Eucharist and at the Second Coming - in order to heal and judge us (1 Cor 11:29).

Scripture talks about this and about nothing but this. Thus, every passage of Scripture talks about how God took flesh to establish the Church and Her sacraments through the four aspects of His Paschal Mystery (Passion, Death, Resurrection and Ascension) and how He will come to judge us on the Last Day. The Incarnation is the foundation upon which these events take place. The Paschal Mystery is the center of the Scriptures.

Logical Consequences: Before, During and After

If the Paschal Mystery is the center of Scripture, a moment's thought reveals that we can therefore slice Scripture up into three sections: the Old Testament (before the Paschal Mystery), the Gospels (the Paschal Mystery itself), and everything after the Gospels (after the Paschal Mystery).

Before: Reading the Old Testament

Every historical event in the Old Testament not only really happened, but each event also symbolically foreshadows some aspect of (a) God's incarnation, (b) the Church, or (c) one or more of Her sacraments.

The four senses are applied most often to the Old Testament historical books, especially the Pentateuch (Genesis, Exodus, Numbers, Leviticus, Deutoronomy), but also to books like 1 and 2 Kings, 1 and 2 Samuel and the like. It is critical to realize that every historical book is prophetic because the events of history prophesy the Incarnation just as thoroughly as the mouths of the prophets did. Thus, every event of salvation history, every aspect of the Temple system of sacrifice, is meant to symbolically describe something about Christ, His Church and His sacraments.

During: Reading about the Paschal Mystery Itself

Every event in Jesus' life (i.e., every event in the Gospels) points either to the Paschal Mystery (Passion, Death, Resurrection and Ascension) or to the Second Coming. This fact is absolutely crucial to understanding the Gospels.

Every event of Jesus' life and ministry is meant to tell us something about the life of the Church and her ministry of the sacraments. Every parable Christ uses portrays the history of how mankind (the Jews and the Gentiles) would react to the First Coming (Jesus and His saving Church) and/or to the Second Coming. Christ's parables aren't just stories about men and women with problems — every parable summarizes huge swaths of salvation history.

After: Reading Acts, the Epistles and Revelation

Every event in the life of the Church after the Ascension points back to the Paschal Mystery that established Her existence. This is particularly true of the lives of the apostles – they all mirror Christ and His saving work in the Paschal Mystery.

Ancillary Principles

Now, given this way of looking at Scripture, we have only two more things to consider. As we do this study and read through examples from the writings of the Fathers and Doctors of the Church, we will notice that their insights were not always identical. Some will interpret a specific event or passage in Scripture in one way; some will read it in another way. If we are to model our interpretations on those of the early Christians, we should follow the example they give us. So, what is their example?

First, each interpretation of a passage should try to account for every element in the passage. The more comprehensive the explanation, the more specific the meanings attached to each element, the better the interpretation is likely to be. Thus, we never attach a generic meaning to a passage (e.g., "The dead bird represents sadness") when a more specific meaning can be assigned (e.g., "Since the dove is a symbol for the Holy Spirit, and death is the separation of soul and body, the death of the bird represents the way our sin separates us from the Holy Spirit").

Second, all the symbolic meanings in the event should come together to form a single image or story. Each aspect of the literal historical event, for instance, should have an attached symbolic meaning. All the meanings should come together to form a single image or message. Sometimes the message has several parts. The more thorough we are in discerning meanings, the clearer the final understanding will be.

Finally, any Scripture interpretation we make is valid as long as it does not violate the teachings of the Church. As we shall see, the early Christians often had widely divergent opinions on what a specific passage of Scripture signified. However, even when they differed, their interpretations were complementary. That is, all of the interpretations could be true at the same time; each one just describes a different aspect of the human condition and God's way of saving us.

Session 1: The Parable of the Good Samaritan

Setting the Context

We begin the study of Scripture's four-fold sense by studying one of Jesus' parables.

As the introductory pages noted, the Gospels are the center of the Scriptures. The Gospels summarize and complete the Old Testament. They also give a concrete understanding of what is going to happen in the broad sweep of man's history. Together with Sacred Tradition and the Magisterium, the Gospels explain everything; they hold the answers to all of life's questions. Everything that comes before and everything that comes after the Gospels is, in a certain sense, divinely inspired commentary on the life of Christ, the central explanation of everything.

As a result, Jesus' parables tend to have an enormous scope. Nearly all of them look in two directions at once. They explain huge swaths of Old Testament history while also giving a rich understanding of what is to come, what human history all means, why everything happens as it does.

The earliest Christians found the parable of the Good Samaritan a marvelously rich canvas, a story that summed up the whole wonderful history of mankind in just a few lines. See how much of the richness you can capture!

Scripture

Luke 10:29-33

But he, wanting to justify himself, said to Jesus, "And who is my neighbor?"

And Jesus answering said,

"A certain man went down from Jerusalem to Jericho, and fell among thieves, which stripped him of his raiment, and wounded him, and departed, leaving him half dead. And by chance there came down a certain Priest that way: and when he saw him, he passed by on the other side. And likewise a Levite, when he was at the place, came and looked on him, and passed by on the other side.

But a certain Samaritan, as he journeyed, came where he was; and when he saw him, he had compassion on him, and went to him, and bound up his wounds, pouring in oil and wine, and set him on his own beast, and brought him to an inn, and took care of him, And on the morrow when he departed, he took out two pence, and gave them to the host, and said to him, Take care of him; and whatsoever you spend more, when I come again, I will repay you."

"Which now of these three, think you, was neighbor to him that fell among the thieves?"

And he said, "He that showed mercy on him."

Then said Jesus to him, "Go, and do likewise."

Questions for Careful Reading

To begin, read through all of the questions before you try to answer the first one. Once you do begin to answer, don't be concerned if you can't answer all the questions. Answer what you can.

In order to answer several of the questions given below, we must first learn about the "matched pair."

Scripture often shows two or three objects or people acting together as one, or two or three things acting in the same way. When this happens, those people or things tend to either:

(a) represent different aspects of a single thing or

(b) represent two things that go together.

For example, when given a matched pair, the Fathers of the Church often assumed God intended the pair to represent one of the following:

- The Law and the Prophets
- The Jews and the Gentiles
- The virtues and the vices
- The Old Law and the New Law
- Works and faith
- The natural and the supernatural
- The Old and the New Testaments
- The Sacraments and the Scripture
- The Church and the Sacraments

This list is by no means exhaustive. The early Christians were quite adept at coming up with pairs or triplets of things that went together. Indeed, if you spent a few moments in thought, you could probably come up with some of the other pairings that they used.

The matched pair is one of the most useful ways to discern the four senses, since it "opens up" the meaning of many passages that would otherwise be hard to understand. With this in mind, let's begin.

1) Keeping in mind that this parable is not just a parable about an Old Testament event, but the whole sweep of human history, who is the "certain man" who was injured? Who injured him?

2) The Priest and the Levite acted in similar ways, so they may be considered a "matched pair." Consider the list of possible matches given above and spend some time thinking about other possible matches. Which, if any, would apply here, or is there another pairing you know that you would like to use? In other words, who or what do the Priest and the Levite represent?

3) The Samaritan acted differently than the Priest and the Levite, so he's not part of the match. Who or what does the Samaritan represent?

4) The innkeeper and the inn are the common destination through which the Samaritan expects the man to be healed. Who or what does the matched pair of the innkeeper and his inn represent?

5) There are at least two more matched pairs we can find in the story (Hint: Consider what the Samaritan uses). What are these other two matched pairs? What might each of them represent? Keep in mind the different ways in which the Samaritan uses each one.

6) There is one thing used by the Samaritan in a unique way, although it complements the two matched pairs discussed in question #4. What might the beast that belonged to the Good Samaritan represent?

Bonus Question

7) Given all of this, what significance might you attach to the starting and ending points of the injured man's journey?

A Guide to the Reading

It takes a certain amount of free association to come up with the answers, and as we shall see, the Fathers themselves had different opinions concerning what each of the elements in this story represent. You and I don't have to match the Fathers precisely; that isn't the point. What matters is that we offer a self-consistent and coherent interpretation that covers as many elements in the passage as we can and that is not at variance with any teaching of the Church. If we have done this, we have a valid interpretation.

Now, what are the elements? During this first study, we will focus on the nouns in the story, even though this limits the interpretation. The Fathers used every element of the story when they gave an interpretation. They looked at the verbs, the historical backgrounds of the various players in the passage under study, the cultural contexts and habits embedded in those backgrounds, etc. That's why they are the masters and we are the students. We will just focus on the easiest aspects, the basic interpretations made possible through studying the nouns and a verb or two.

So, in this case, we focus on the man, the priest, the Levite, the Samaritan, the wine, the oil, the beast, the innkeeper and the coins. The nouns drive the interpretation. Later on in this course, we will see that the meanings of place names also often play an absolutely critical role in interpretation, but we will disregard them in this first example.

Below is a summary of how various Doctors and Fathers of the Church interpreted the different elements in the parable of the Good Samaritan. Notice that no one incorporated every element – each of these brilliant commentators took as much as he could to form his explanation.

Similarly, as you can see, the Fathers did not always agree on exactly what a symbol meant. What is interesting is that their answers complement one another - in most cases, all of the answers given could be simultaneously true. As long as your solution does not violate a doctrine of the Church, it is perfectly acceptable.

The certain man

The whole human race: Thomas Aquinas.

Adam: Augustine, Chrysostom

Human nature: Theophylact

Our neighbor: Augustine

Jerusalem (the name means "site of peace")

Eden: Augustine

Heavenly Paradise: Pseudo-Augustine

The descent into the valley

The Fall: Augustine

Jericho (the name means "moon")

Human mortality – it waxes and wanes: Augustine

The world – all things born will die: Pseudo-Augustine

Thieves

The devil, armed with malice and guile: Chrysostom

Angels of darkness: Ambrose, Augustine

Stripped clothes

Virtue: Augustine

Immortality: Augustine

Grace: Ambrose, Basil

Wounded, half-dead state

Free Will: Augustine, Pseudo-Augustine

Sin: Augustine, Basil, Venerable Bede, Chrysostom

Immortal soul/mortal body = half-dead: Theophylact
Human hope in Christ's salvation = half-dead: Theophylact

The Priest (neighbor by birth)
Aaron (and his sacrifices): Chrysostom
The Law: Augustine, Theophylact

The Levite (neighbor by birth)
Moses (and his law): Chrysostom
The Prophets: Augustine

Samaritan (far removed by birth, the word means "keeper")
Jesus, who descended from heaven (Jerusalem): Augustine,
Thomas Aquinas, Ambrose

Came near
Incarnation: Augustine, Thomas Aquinas, Ambrose

Binding the wounds
Saves us from sin: Augustine
New Law: Ambrose

Oil
Good hope through reconciliation: Augustine
Remission of sin: Ambrose
Softness of mercy (gentleness): Gregory the Great
Commune with men via Christ's human nature: Theophylact
Baptismal Chrism: Chrysostom

Wine
Incitement to work in the Spirit: Augustine
Judgement: Ambrose
Sharp constraint washing corruption away: Gregory the Great

Commune with God via Christ's divine nature: Theophylact
Blood of His Passion: Chrysostom

His beast
Our flesh: Augustine, Ambrose
Jesus' Body: Theophylact

Placed on the beast
Belief in the Incarnation: Augustine
Christ bears the sins of man: Ambrose
Baptism (it brings us into the Church): Bede

Inn
The Church: Theophylact, Chrysostom, Bede

Innkeeper
The Apostle Paul: Augustine
Christian faithful: Ambrose

The next day
The Resurrection: Ambrose

Two pence
Two covenants, Old and New: Ambrose
Two commandments of love: Augustine
Promise of present life and life to come: Augustine
The sacraments: Origen

Questions for Application

1) The questions above show us that the parable explains the whole sweep of salvation history. But Scripture always applies to every age. How does this way of understanding the parable change the way you apply this parable to your own life right now?

2) We are often asked how we can be Good Samaritans. We are not often asked how we are like the injured man. How does putting yourself in the place of the injured man affect your understanding of the importance of Jesus and His Church in your life?

3) Try re-reading the parable from the perspective of the injured man, but using different combinations of the meanings given above. How does each different combination affect your appreciation of the different elements of Catholic Faith?

Approach to Prayer

Pray Psalm 78:1-32.
Pause for silent reflection.
End by praying Luke 1:39-45 together.

For Individual Reading: *St. Augustine*

Now when deep reflection had drawn up out of the secret depths of my soul all my misery and had heaped it up before the sight of my heart, there arose a mighty storm, accompanied by a mighty rain of tears. That I might give way fully to my tears and lamentations, I stole away from [my friend] Alypius, for it seemed to me that solitude was more appropriate for the business of weeping. I went far enough away that I could feel that even his presence was no restraint upon me. This was the way I felt at the time, and he realized it. I suppose I had said something before I started up and he noticed that the sound of my voice was choked with weeping. And so he stayed alone, where we had been sitting together, greatly astonished. I flung myself down under a fig tree — how I know not — and gave free course to my tears. The streams of my eyes gushed out an acceptable sacrifice to thee. And, not indeed in these words, but to this effect, I cried to thee: "And thou, O Lord, how long? How long, O Lord? Wilt thou be angry forever? Oh, remember not against us our former iniquities." For I felt that I was still enthralled by them. I sent up these sorrowful cries: "How long, how long? Tomorrow and tomorrow? Why not now? Why not this very hour make an end to my uncleanness?"

I was saying these things and weeping in the most bitter contrition of my heart, when suddenly I heard the voice of a boy or a girl — I know not which — coming from the neighboring house, chanting over and over again, "Pick it up, read it; pick it up, read it."

Immediately I ceased weeping and began most earnestly to think whether it was usual for children in some kind of game to sing such a song, but I could not remember ever having heard the like. So, damming the torrent of my tears, I got to my feet, for I could not but think that this was a divine command to open the Bible and read the first passage I should light upon. For I had heard how Anthony, accidentally coming into church while the Gospel was being read, received the admonition as if what was read had been addressed to him: "Go and sell what you have and give it to the poor, and you shall have treasure in heaven; and come and follow me" (Matt 19:21). By such an oracle he was forthwith converted to thee.

So I quickly returned to the bench where Alypius was sitting, for there I had put down the apostle's book when I had left there. I snatched it up, opened it, and in silence read the paragraph on which my eyes first fell: "Not in rioting and drunkenness, not in chambering and wantonness, not in strife and envying, but put on the Lord Jesus Christ, and make no provision for the flesh to fulfill the lusts thereof" (Romans 13:13). I wanted to read no further, nor did I need to. For instantly, as the sentence ended, there was infused in my heart something like the light of full certainty and all the gloom of doubt vanished away.

Closing the book, then, and putting my finger or something else for a mark I began — now with a tranquil countenance — to tell it all to Alypius. And he in turn disclosed to me what had been going on in himself, of which I knew nothing. He asked to see what I had read. I showed him, and he looked on even further than I had read. I had not known what followed. But indeed it was this, "Him that is weak in the faith, receive" (Romans 14:1). This he applied to himself, and told me so. By these words of warning he was strengthened, and by exercising his good resolution and purpose — all very much in keeping with his character, in which, in these respects, he was always far different from and better than I — he joined me in full commitment without any restless hesitation.

Then we went in to my mother, and told her what happened, to her great joy. We explained to her how it had occurred — and she leaped for joy triumphant; and she blessed thee, who art "able to do exceedingly abundantly above all that we ask or think" (Ephesians 3:20). For she saw that thou hadst granted her far more than she had ever asked for in all her pitiful and doleful lamentations. For thou didst so convert me to thee that I sought neither a wife nor any other of this world's hopes, but set my feet on that rule of faith which so many years before thou hadst showed her in her dream about me. And so thou didst turn her grief into gladness more plentiful than she had ventured to desire, and dearer and purer than the desire she used to cherish of having grandchildren of my flesh.

- From Augustine's *Confessions*, Book 8, Chapter 12

Session 2: The Healing of Leprosy

Setting the Context

In the first assignment, we saw how the nouns in one of Christ's parables could point us towards a deeper typological understanding of Scripture. In this second assignment, we will not only study the nouns, we will spend some time with the verbs as well. Not only every person, place and thing, but also every action in the Old Testament was meant to be a lived typology pointing to the fulfillment in the New Testament.

Further, in the first assignment, we saw the use of matched pairs, two things which are generally thought of together. In this assignment, we will see a different principle at work: A single thing is represented by spreading its qualities across multiple actors. In this method of representation, which could be called the the "Simon of Cyrene" principle, several different objects are meant to be taken together, each carrying part of the load. When this is done, we see that all of them together represent a single object, event or person.

One final word: Keep in mind that the Scripture passage you are about to read accurately describes exactly how the Hebrews handled the problem of leprosy for a thousand years. You are reading history, but it is also prophecy, a prophecy that is acted out through the typological meanings associated with the liturgical actions you study.

Scripture

Leviticus 14:1-20

And the Lord spoke to Moses, saying, "This is the rite of a leper, when he is to be cleansed: he shall be brought to the priest who is to go out of the camp and having determined that the leprosy is cleansed, shall command him that is to be purified, to offer for himself two living sparrows, which it is lawful to eat, and cedar wood, and scarlet, and hyssop. And he shall command one of the sparrows to be immolated in an earthen vessel over living waters.

But the other that is alive he shall dip, with the cedar wood, and the scarlet and the hyssop, in the blood of the sparrow that is immolated: Wherewith he shall sprinkle him that is to be cleansed seven times, that he may be rightly purified: and he shall let go the living sparrow, that it may fly into the field. And when the man hath washed his clothes, he shall shave all the hair of his body, and shall be washed with water: and being purified, he shall enter into the camp, yet he must remain outside his own tent seven days: And on the seventh day he shall shave the hair of his head, and his beard and his eyebrows, and the hair of all his body.

And having washed again his clothes, and his body, on the eighth day he shall take two lambs without blemish, and an ewe of a year old without blemish, and three tenths of flour tempered with oil for a sacrifice, and a sextary of oil apart. And when the priest that purifieth the man, hath presented him, and all these things before the Lord, at the door of the tent of meeting, he shall take a lamb, and offer it for a trespass offering with the sextary of oil: and having offered all before the Lord, he shall immolate the lamb, and the holocaust, where the victim for sin is usually to be immolated, that is, in the holy place: for as the sin offering, like the victim for a trespass offering belongs to the priest: it is the holy of holies.

And the priest taking of the blood of the victim that was immolated for trespass, shall put it upon the tip of the right ear of him that is cleansed, and upon the thumb of his right hand and the great toe of his right foot: And he shall pour of the sextary of oil into his own left hand, and shall dip his right finger in it, and sprinkle it before the Lord seven times. And the rest of the oil in his left band, he shall pour upon the tip of the right ear of him that is cleansed, and upon the thumb of his right hand and the great toe of his right foot, and upon the blood that was shed for trespass, and upon his head. And he shall pray for him before the Lord, and shall offer the sacrifice for sin: then shall he immolate the holocaust, and put it on the altar with the libations, and the man shall be rightly cleansed.

Questions for Careful Reading

Read through all the questions first, then answer whichever of the following questions that you can:

1) What does leprosy signify?

2) What does the camp signify (the leper must remain outside the camp until declared clean and purified)?

3) Who or what does the priest represent?

4) What do the birds represent (consider them multiple aspects of one thing)?

5) What does the earthen vessel represent (Hint: If you aren't sure, you can do a word search on "earthen vessels" in an electronic Bible to help nail down the meaning)?

6) What does the water represent?

7) What do the cedar wood, scarlet yarn and hyssop together represent (consider them multiple aspects of one thing)?

8) Why does the man wash his garments and shave off his hair? He is in the camp but outside his tent for a total of eight days. Why is that number of days important?

9) What does the lamb's blood represent, and why is it placed as it is on the former leper's body (see Leviticus 8:6-13, 23)?

10) What does the oil represent?

11) What does the seven-fold sprinkling represent?

12) Why are the lamb and the cereal offering offered together (again, consider them multiple aspects of the same thing)?

A Guide to the Reading

Keep in mind that the principles we use to study this particular Levitical sacrifice can be repeated with every one of the Levitical sacrifices. Indeed, Thomas Aquinas does exactly this kind of analysis in the *Summa Theologica*, in the section on the Treatise on Law, when he discusses the ceremonial sacrifices.

Justin Martyr's interpretation:

By the two birds Christ is denoted, both dead as man, and living as God. He is likened to a bird, because He is understood and declared to be from above, and from heaven. And the living bird, having been dipped in the blood of the dead one, was afterwards let go. For the living and divine Word was in the crucified and dead temple [of the body], as being a partaker of the passion, and yet impossible to God.

By that which took place in the running water, in which the wood and the hyssop and the scarlet were dipped, is set forth the bloody passion of Christ on the cross for the salvation of those who are sprinkled with the Spirit, and the water, and the blood. This is why the material for purification was not provided chiefly with reference to leprosy, but with regard to the forgiveness of sins, that both leprosy might be understood to be an emblem of sin, and the things which were sacrificed an emblem of Him who was to be sacrificed for sins.

For this reason, consequently, he ordered that the scarlet should be dipped at the same time in the water, thus predicting that the flesh should no longer possess its natural [evil] properties [but be cleansed by baptismal water]. For this reason, also, were there the two birds, the one being sacrificed in the water, and the other dipped both in the blood and in the water and then sent away, just as is narrated also respecting the goats. [see Colossians 2:12, "buried with Him in baptism, you rise with Him through faith in the working of God, who raised Him from the dead."]

The goat that was sent away presented a type of Him who takes away the sins of men. But the two contained a representation of the one economy of God incarnate. For He was wounded for our transgressions, and He bore the sins of many, and He was delivered for our iniquities.

Additional notes:

The former leper, having been baptized by the blood of the dove killed over running water, is anointed with that blood as if he were a priest, for our baptism consecrates us as priests, prophets and kings.

The number eight was significant in this reading because Jesus died on the sixth day (Friday), spent the seventh day in the tomb (Saturday) and rose on the eighth day (Sunday). For this reason, eight almost always symbolizes resurrection and new life in the Old Testament.

If you ever visit churches in Europe, you will often see a building ouside the church called a baptistry. Unbaptized adults were not permitted to enter a church. The baptistry was set apart from the church as the building where the unbaptized received the sacrament of baptism, and thus the right to enter the church and the Mass itself . It typically had eight sides in order to signify the rebirth of resurrection Christ gave to us on the eighth day. For this reason, even modern baptismal fonts typically have eight sides.

Questions for Application

1) When has your sin made you feel like a leper?

2) Compare how you might feel if you were confronted by a leper to how you feel when confronted with the confessional. How are the two reactions similar? How are they different? Why might this be the case?

3) The dove and the lamb were killed despite their innocence. When have you been unjustly accused? How did you react? Compare your reaction to Jesus' reaction to unjust accusations.

Approach to Prayer

Pray Proverbs 1:1-6 together.
Pause for silent reflection.
End by praying together Proverbs 2:1-8.

For Individual Reading: *Thomas Aquinas*

What is the Summa Theologica?

Many people don't know that the *Summa Theologica* was meant to be an introductory theology text for incoming seminary students. In the *Summa*, Aquinas taught the importance of learning to do typological interpretations of Scripture. Below is his commentary on the reason we can use these principles when we interpret the ceremonial law in the Old Testament.

"As stated above (in Article 1, Question 99, Articles 3, 4), the ceremonial precepts are those which refer to the worship of God. Now the Divine worship is twofold: internal, and external. For since man is composed of soul and body, each of these should be applied to the worship of God; the soul by an interior worship; the body by an outward worship: hence it is written (Psalm 83:3): "My heart and my flesh have rejoiced in the living God." And as the body is ordained to God through the soul, so the outward worship is ordained to the internal worship. Now interior worship consists in the soul being united to God by the intellect and affections. Which is why, according to the various ways in which the intellect and affections of the man who worships God are rightly united to God, his external actions are applied in various ways to the Divine worship."

"For in the state of future bliss, the human intellect will gaze on the Divine Truth in Itself. Which is why the external worship will not consist in anything figurative, but solely in the praise of God, proceeding from the inward knowledge and affection, according to Is. 51:3: "Joy and gladness shall be found therein, thanksgiving and the voice of praise."

"But in the present state of life, we are unable to gaze on the Divine Truth in Itself, and we need the ray of Divine light to shine upon us under the form of certain created objects which our senses can grasp, as Dionysius states; we perceive these objects in various ways, however, according to the various states of human knowledge. For under the Old Law, neither was the Divine Truth manifest in Itself, nor was the way leading to that manifestation as yet opened out, as the Apostle declares (Hebrews 9:8). Hence the external worship of the Old Law needed to be figurative, it prophesied not only the future truth to be manifested in our heavenly country, but also of Christ, Who is the way leading to that heavenly manifestation. But under the New Law this way is already fully revealed, and therefore it needs no longer to be foreshadowed as something future, but to be brought to our minds as something past or present. The truth of the glory to come, which is not yet revealed, is the only thing that needs to be foreshadowed. This is what the Apostle says (Hebrews 11:1): "The Law has a shadow of the good things to come, not the very image of the things": for a shadow is less than an image. The image belongs to the New Law, but the shadow belongs to the Old."

- *Summa Theologica*, First Part of the Second Part,
   Question 101

Session 3: Samuel Anoints David

Setting the Context

In the second session, we saw how a grouping of things could come together to form a single thing (e.g. the cedar wood, scarlet yarn and hyssop together representing the Passion: the wood of the cross, the blood of Christ and the thirst for souls).

Now we will see how pivotal a place name can be. In 1 Samuel 16:1-12, the key bit of knowledge is the meaning of the word "Bethlehem" – it means "House of Bread."

Similarly, the Greek word for "thanksgiving" is "eucharisis." The description given by Samuel of the kind of feast he will offer matches the description given in Leviticus 3:1 and Leviticus 7:11-22 for the peace offering, the *eucharasis*. It is an offering given at the fulfillment of a vow, the only sacrifice in which a group of friends may be invited to partake of the sacrificial feast.

Scripture Reading

1 Samuel 16:1-12

The LORD said to Samuel: "How long will you grieve for Saul, whom I have rejected as king of Israel? Fill your horn with oil, and be on your way. I am sending you to Jesse of Bethlehem, for I have chosen my king from among his sons." But Samuel replied: "How can I go? Saul will hear of it and kill me." To this the LORD answered: "Take a heifer along and say, 'I have come to sacrifice to the LORD.' Invite Jesse to the sacrifice, and I myself will tell you what to do; you are to anoint for me the one I point out to you." Samuel did as the LORD had commanded him.

When he entered Bethlehem, the elders of the city came trembling to meet him and inquired, "Is your visit peaceful, O seer?" He replied: "Yes! I have come to sacrifice to the LORD. So cleanse yourselves and join me today for the banquet." He also had Jesse and his sons cleanse themselves and invited them to the sacrifice. As they came, he looked at Eliab and thought, "Surely the LORD'S anointed is here before him." But the LORD said to Samuel: "Do not judge from his appearance or from his lofty stature, because I have rejected him. Not as man sees does God see, because man sees the appearance but the LORD looks into the heart."

Then Jesse called Abinadab and presented him before Samuel, who said, "The Lord has not chosen him." Next Jesse presented Shammah, but Samuel said, "The LORD has not chosen this one either." In the same way Jesse presented seven sons before Samuel, but Samuel said to Jesse, "The LORD has not chosen any one of these." Then Samuel asked Jesse, "Are these all the sons you have?" Jesse replied, "There is still the youngest, who is tending the sheep." Samuel said to Jesse, "Send for him; we will not begin the sacrificial banquet until he arrives here." Jesse sent and had the young man brought to them. He was ruddy, a youth handsome to behold and making a splendid appearance. The LORD said, "There—anoint him, for this is he!"

Questions for Careful Reading

Read 1 Samuel 16:1-12 above. Replace every occurrence of the word "Bethlehem" in the above passage with "House of Bread." Then read through all the questions before you attempt to answer any of them.

Hint: Once you can answer the last question, the first six questions are easier to answer.

1) What is the significance of requiring the elders to cleanse themselves before they come to the feast?

2) What is the New Testament lesson Samuel learns from looking at Eliab?

3) What is the number of the youngest son and why is his number significant (refer to lesson 2, if necessary)?

4) Why is the profession of this son significant (e.g., see Ezekiel 34:2-10)?

5) Why is the sacrificial banquet delayed until this son arrives? What does this point to?

6) What New Testament fulfillment is this passage talking about? That is, what New Testament fulfillment does Samuel's sacrifice point to?

A Guide to the Reading

One of the best ways to "see" typology at work is to study how the liturgical readings are organized in the Catholic liturgy. There is an ancient rule in the Church, "Lex orandi, lex credendi", which translated means "the law of prayer is the law of belief" or "we pray what we believe."

Thus, noticing where a particular Scripture falls in the reading cycle and seeing what other readings are arranged with it can be of great assistance in accurately determining what a passage means.

1 Samuel 16:1-12 appears twice in the cycle. It appears first on the 4th Sunday of Lent, Cycle A. The readings for the day are:

- 1 Sam 16:1, 6-7, 10-13 — David is anointed king.

- Ps 23:1-3a, 3b-4, 5, 6 — The Lord is my shepherd, I shall not want... He sets a table.

- Eph 5:8-14 — Do not take part in works of darkness, be children of the light.

- John 9:1-41 or 9:1, 6-9, 13-17, 34-38 — Jesus heals the man blind from birth.

It appears again on Tuesday of the second week in Ordinary Time during Year II of the readings. The day's readings are:

- 1 Sam 16:1-13 — David is anointed king.

- Ps 89:20, 21-22, 27-28 — God anointed David and will keep covenant with him.

- Mark 2:23-28 — The apostles eat wheat from the fields as David ate the showbread from the Temple.

Both contexts are quite telling, each stressing a different aspect of 1 Samuel 16. The Sunday Psalm reading and the Tuesday Gospel reading are the most immediately helpful in this particular typological interpretation, although the Sunday Gospel reading is quite helpful in answering (2).

The name "Bethlehem" means "House of Bread." Samuel is going to the House of Bread to find the King who is to be consecrated. From this king's line will come the Messiah.

Note the kind of sacrificial banquet Samuel offers - this is the fulfillment banquet spoken of in Leviticus, the *eucharasis*. All must be ritually clean to participate, just as we must be cleansed by Reconciliation before we participate in the Eucharist.

The very first person Samuel sees seems good to him. Samuel is ready to consecrate the eldest son king. But God stops him. We are not to judge by appearance when searching out the son of Jesse, the anointed King who resides in the House of Bread. We find the King only when we see as God sees, because man sees only the appearance, but God knows the heart of everything. This foreshadows the Real Presence of Christ in the Eucharist under the appearance of bread and wine, i.e., it is a foreshadowing of transubstantiation.

Kings were often referred to as "shepherds of the people" by sources ranging from Homer (7th century BC) through Hesychius (5th century AD), and Holy Scripture follows this tradition. See, for example:

- Num 27:16-17 "Let the LORD, the God of the spirits of all flesh, appoint a man over the congregation, 17 who shall go out before them and come in before them, who shall lead them out and bring them in; that the congregation of the LORD may not be as sheep which have no shepherd."

- 2 Sam 5:2 "In times past, when Saul was king over us, it was you that led out and brought in Israel; and the LORD said to you, 'You shall be shepherd of my people Israel, and you shall be prince over Israel.'"

- Jer 31:10 "Hear the word of the LORD, O nations, and declare it in the coastlands afar off; say, 'He who scattered Israel will gather him, and will keep him as a shepherd keeps his flock.'"

- Ezek 34:23-24 "And I will set up over them one shepherd, my servant David, and he shall feed them: he shall feed them and be their shepherd. 24 And I, the LORD, will be their God, and my servant David shall be prince among them; I, the LORD, have spoken.

- Zech 10:2-3 "For the teraphim utter nonsense, and the diviners see lies; the dreamers tell false dreams, and give empty consolation. Therefore the people wander like sheep; they are afflicted for want of a shepherd. My anger is hot against the shepherds, and I will punish the leaders; for the LORD of hosts cares for his flock, the house of Judah, and will make them like his proud steed in battle."

Seven sons passed by; it was the eighth who was anointed king. Christ will rise after three days in the tomb, but He will not arise on the seventh day, the Sabbath. He rises on the eighth day, the day of New Creation.

Questions for Application

1) How is Jesus, hidden in the Eucharist, like Jesus, hidden in the Old Testament Scriptures? Has this week's study given you a deeper appreciation for the Eucharist?

2) When have you felt like Samuel — knowing that God wants you to do something, but afraid of the consequences? Was Jesus hidden in your situation also?

3) When have you had difficulty explaining the Eucharist to someone? Would knowing about this passage and this method of reading Scripture have been helpful to you?

4) Catholics often like to re-create the Seder meal for a parish event, but very few attempt to re-create the Old Testament *eucharasis*, with its slaughter and ritual consumption of a heifer. Why is the sacrificial aspect of the Eucharist de-emphasized today? What consequences follow from this changed emphasis?

Approach to Prayer

Pray Matthew 12:42.
Pause for silent meditation.
Close by praying Matthew 26:26-30.

For Individual Reading: *Our Lady of Guadalupe*

Bishop Zumarraga, the bishop over the Spanish holdings in Mexico, had a serious problem. Led by their Spanish administrators, Spanish soldiers treated the natives as subhuman cattle. They exploited, enslaved and killed thousands. When priests tried to intervene, they too were beaten or killed. The people began to rebel. Bishop Zumarraga smuggled a message in a hollowed-out crucifix to Charles V, King of Spain, asking for new administrators to correct the injustice. As he waited months in Mexico for the long sea voyage to bring the king's reply, he asked Mary for help, and for Castilian roses as a sign his prayers had been heard.

On Saturday, Dec. 9, 1531, Juan Diego was crossing Tepeyac hill to go to Mass. This hill had once borne a temple dedicated to the Aztec goddess Tonatzin, one of the few Aztec deities who did not ask for human sacrifice. Suddenly, he heard a heavenly choir, and a woman's voice calling, "Juanito, Juan Dieguito." As he followed the voice to the top of the hill, he met a beautiful woman who called herself the Perpetual Virgin Mary, Mother of the True God.

Speaking in Nahuatl, the Aztec language, she told Juan to inform the bishop that a church should be built on this hill and dedicated to her. Juan walked to the city and told the bishop, but the bishop did not believe him.

As Juan returned home, he again saw the lady at Tepeyac. She told him to revisit the bishop and then meet her on the hill on the evening of the next day. The following morning, he returned to the bishop. The bishop told Juan to bring a sign from the woman and sent him away, but sent a few men to follow him. The searchers lost Juan in the hills so they returned and told the bishop Juan lied.

Meanwhile, on his return home, Juan found his uncle desperately ill. He spent the entire day caring for his uncle, but to no avail. He became more and more ill with each passing hour. As the sun set, his dying uncle begged Juan to bring a priest to hear his confession. Juan headed back towards town, but as he walked, he realized he had neglected his appointed meeting with the lady. Because he knew how important it was for his dying uncle to receive the sacrament of Anointing of the Sick, he skirted around the edge of Tepayac hill instead of taking the shorter route over the top: He didn't want to be slowed down by meeting the lady. Holding a long conversation with the lady, or worse, being sent on another mission from her, might prevent his uncle from dying in the graces of the Church.

As he walked around the hill the lady floated down to him, and Juan, embarrassed, explained why he was late. She told him his uncle was cured and asked him to go to the top of the hill to collect roses there. To his surprise, he found dozens of out-of-season, dew-covered roses in bloom among the frost and rocks on the hilltop. He gathered the roses in his tilma, the cactus-fiber cloak he wore, and brought them to the lady, who arranged them in the cloak for him.

He returned to the bishop with the roses wrapped in his tilma and found the bishop in conversation with the new governor of Mexico, who had just arrived. When he dropped the edge of his tilma, the bishop gasped in surprise - these were Castilian roses tumbling out onto the ground! Then all the men in the room dropped to their knees at the sight of an even greater surprise: an image of the Virgin Mary had suddenly appeared, impressed upon the tilma!

The bishop accepted the tilma as the sign he had prayed for, and Juan returned home to find his uncle had indeed been cured by a beautiful woman who called herself "The Lady Tecoatlaxopeuh," (pronounced "tekwetlasupe," which sounded to the Spaniards like "de Guadalupe"). This Nahuatl word means the Lady "who crushes the stone serpent." Quetzalcoatl, who demanded human sacrifice, was the stone serpent god. Within ten years, 10 million pagan Aztecs either made pilgrimage to the image or heard the descriptions of those who had, and accepted Christianity in the largest and most rapid conversion ever recorded. She became the national symbol for Mexico, the patroness of the Americas.

- From *Artfully Teaching the Faith*, "Our Lady of Guadalupe"

Session 4: Elijah and the Pagan Priests

Setting the Context

In the third session, we saw how the place name "Bethlehem," meaning "House of Bread", oriented the entire passage towards a foreshadowing of the Eucharist. We also saw how the use of the number "eight" enriched this foreshadowing.

In typological interpretation, numbers often play an important role. Since Jesus was crucified on a Friday (the sixth day) and His Body was in the tomb while He preached to those in the underworld on the Sabbath (the seventh day), it can be said that He rose on the eighth day (Sunday). Thus, the number eight always symbolizes Christ's resurrection. Many ancient baptismal buildings and fonts are eight-sided because we are baptized into His death and His resurrection (I once saw a six-sided baptismal font, clearly built by an architect who had never been taught typology – the priests who pastored at that parish were rather chagrined over the error).

In this week's passage, we will see a more complex foreshadowing. How many different elements of Catholic liturgy and sacrament do you see foreshadowed in this passage?

Note also that this passage is the earliest recorded example of someone using the scientific method. In the scientific method, the seeker investigates reality by creating two identical situations: a test situation and a control. He changes one element in the test situation and observes how that changed element affects the results. Another example of this can be found in the story of Gideon and the fleece (Judges 6:37-40).

Scripture Reading

1 Kings 18:20-40

So Ahab sent to all the Israelites and had the prophets assemble on Mount Carmel. Elijah appealed to all the people and said, "How long will you straddle the issue? If the LORD is God, follow him; if Baal, follow him." The people, however, did not answer him. So Elijah said to the people, "I am the only surviving prophet of the LORD, and there are four hundred and fifty prophets of Baal. Give us two young bulls. Let them choose one, cut it into pieces, and place it on the wood, but start no fire. I shall prepare the other and place it on the wood, but shall start no fire. You shall call on your gods, and I will call on the LORD. The God who answers with fire is God." All the people answered, "Agreed!"

Elijah then said to the prophets of Baal, "Choose one young bull and prepare it first, for there are more of you. Call upon your gods, but do not start the fire." Taking the young bull that was turned over to them, they prepared it and called on Baal from morning to noon, saying, "Answer us, Baal!" But there was no sound, and no one answering. And they hopped around the altar they had prepared. When it was noon, Elijah taunted them: "Call louder, for he is a god and may be meditating, or may have retired, or may be on a journey. Perhaps he is asleep and must be awakened."

They called out louder and slashed themselves with swords and spears, as was their custom, until blood gushed over them. Noon passed and they remained in a prophetic state until the time for offering sacrifice. But there was not a sound; no one answered, and no one was listening.

Then Elijah said to all the people, "Come here to me." When they had done so, he repaired the altar of the LORD which had been destroyed. He took twelve stones, for the number of tribes of the sons of Jacob, to whom the LORD had said, "Your name shall be Israel." He built an altar in honor of the LORD with the stones, and made a trench around the altar large enough for two seahs of grain. When he had arranged the wood, he cut up the young bull and laid it on the wood. "Fill four jars with water," he said, "and pour it over the holocaust and over the wood." "Do it again," he said, and they did it again. "Do it a third time," he said, and they did it a third time. The water flowed around the altar, and the trench was filled with the water. At the time for offering sacrifice, the prophet Elijah came forward and said, "LORD, God of Abraham, Isaac, and Israel, let it be known this day that you are God in Israel and that I am your servant and have done all these things by your command. Answer me, LORD! Answer me, that this people may know that you, LORD, are God and that you have brought them back to their senses."

The LORD'S fire came down and consumed the holocaust, wood, stones, and dust, and it lapped up the water in the trench. Seeing this, all the people fell prostrate and said, "The LORD is God! The LORD is God!" Then Elijah said to them, "Seize the prophets of Baal. Let none of them escape!" They were seized, and Elijah had them brought down to the brook Kishon and there he slit their throats.

Questions for Careful Reading

We will study 1 Kings 18:30-40, concentrating on what Elijah did and what happened.

1) What is the significance of the trench that can hold two seahs of grain? (Hint: The Hebrew word "trench" also means "a bandage or plaster, as placed upon a wound" and thus can mean "healing").

2) What might the two seahs of grain represent?

3) What is the significance of the four jars of water?

4) What is the significance of washing the altar with the three-fold washing?

5) What is the significance of the altar being totally consumed by fire from heaven?

6) What is the significance of Elijah having the pagan prophets slain by the brook? (Hint: In earlier times, a pond or lake was referred to as "still water" because it didn't move, while a brook, stream or river was called "living water" because it did.)

If you read farther, you will see more typological significance in the verses immediately following the passage under study. Feel free to comment on those passages as well, if you want.

A Guide to the Reading

Here is one possible interpretation:

Elijah builds the altar on a foundation of twelve stones, the foundation of the twelve tribes of Israel and the twelve Apostles.

The trench represents the enormous gulf between God and man, healed and thereby overcome by the waters of baptism.

The offering is a bull cut in pieces and laid upon the wood, representing the crucifixion and death of Christ.

The two seahs of grain represent the Old and the New Testaments, the "bread from heaven" Whose life is expressed in the Word of Scripture.

The four jars represent the four Gospels, living waters in the earthen vessels of the Evangelists. The four jars may also be seen as the Gospels being preached to the four corners of the earth. Thus, the sacrifice of the crucifixion enlivens the washing of water with the Word, i.e., baptism leads to Eucharist.

According to Deuteronomy 4:24 and Hebrews 12:29 "Our God is a consuming fire," and tongues of fire descend upon the apostles in Acts 2. Thus, the fire represents the Holy Spirit, Who completely consumes the substance of the sacrifice — bull, wood, water, altar - there remained in its place only divine fire. This prefigures the transubstantiation of the Eucharistic sacrifice of the Mass. In this sacrifice, the people recognize the presence of God.

The prophets of Baal, representing the hold Satan and sin have upon us prior to baptism, are killed by the living waters of the brook, just as the living waters of baptism destroy the sins within us.

Questions for Application

1) When have you tested God?

2) When has God tested you?

3) When Elijah put the question to the Israelites concerning who they would follow, they were afraid to answer, for fear of choosing badly. When have you done that? How did the situation get resolved?

Approach to Prayer

Pray Hebrews 8:1-6.
Pause in silent meditation.
Close by praying the Canticle of Simeon, Luke 2:29-32.

For Individual Reading: *St. Francis of Assisi*

In 1279, at the city of Damietta on the Nila Delta, which the members of the Fourth Crusade were besieging, Francis was deeply shocked at the profligacy, the cynicism, and the lack of discipline of the soldiers of the cross. When in August the leaders prepared to attack, he predicted failure and tried to dissuade them from the attempt. The Christians were driven back with the slaughter of six thousand men, yet they continued the siege, and at last took the city. Meanwhile, a number of the soldiers had pledged themselves to live by Francis' rule.

Francis also paid several visits to the Saracen leader, Melek-el-Kamil, Sultan of Egypt. There is a story to the effect that he first went among the enemy with only Brother Illuminato, calling out, "Sultan! Sultan!" Instead of being killed on the spot, he was captured and brought before the Sultan. When asked his errand, Francis replied boldly, "I am sent by the Most High God, to show you and your people the way of salvation by announcing to you the truths of the Gospel." Discussion followed, and other audiences. The Sultan, somewhat moved, invited Francis to stay with him. "If you and your people," said Francis, "will accept the word of God, I will with joy stay with you. If you yet waver between Christ and Mohammed, order a fire kindled and I will go into it with your priests that you may see which is the true faith." The Sultan replied that he did not think any of his imams would dare to enter the fire. He would not accept Francis' condition for fear of upsetting the people. Indeed, he told Francis, "I would convert to your religion which is a beautiful one — but both of us would be murdered." Instead, he offered him many presents, which Francis refused. Fearing finally that some of his Moslems might desert to the Christians, he sent Francis, under guard, back to the camp.

-Taken from Sabatier, *Life of St. Francis of Assisi*

Session 5: The Finding in the Temple

Setting the Context

Now that we have seen several examples of Old Testament typology, let us move on to New Testament typology. As previously indicated, the shift to the New Testament necessarily shifts the emphasis of the interpretation.

In the Old Testament, everything pointed forward to Jesus, His Church and Her sacramental, liturgical life. In the Gospels, the rules change slightly. As even a quick overview of the Gospels shows, one quarter of each Gospel is devoted to seven days in Jesus' life, describing the Passion, Death, Resurrection and Ascension, the four aspects of the Paschal Mystery. Put another way, the Gospels spend about as much time describing the events of Jesus' last week on earth as they do discussing His entire life prior to that last week. The Gospels are written primarily to provide a context for the Paschal Mystery.

Thus, Jesus' parables generally summarize salvation history in ways that point to the Paschal Mystery, the Second Coming or both. Similarly, the events of Jesus' life point either to the Paschal Mystery He will soon endure or to the Second Coming or to both. The Passion narratives are the culmination of the Gospels, and the Gospels are the culmination of Scripture.

With that in mind, take a look at the finding of the child Jesus in the Temple. By now, you should be able to read through it with typological eyes and begin to see why this passage is often seen as a summary of the Gospels.

Scripture Reading

Luke 2:40-52

The child grew and became strong, filled with wisdom; and the favor of God was upon him. Each year his parents went to Jerusalem for the feast of Passover, and when he was twelve years old, they went up according to festival custom. After they had completed its days, as they were returning, the boy Jesus remained behind in Jerusalem, but his parents did not know it.

Thinking that he was in the caravan, they journeyed for a day and looked for him among their relatives and acquaintances, but not finding him, they returned to Jerusalem to look for him. After three days they found him in the temple, sitting in the midst of the teachers, listening to them and asking them questions, and all who heard him were astounded at his understanding and his answers. When his parents saw him, they were astonished, and his mother said to him, "Son, why have you done this to us? Your father and I have been looking for you with great anxiety." And he said to them, "Why were you looking for me? Did you not know that I must be in my Father's house?" But they did not understand what he said to them.

He went down with them and came to Nazareth, and was obedient to them; and his mother kept all these things in her heart. And Jesus advanced (in) wisdom and age and favor before God and man.

Questions for Careful Reading

1) Each year Jesus' parents went to Jerusalem for Passover. What other part of the Gospels describe Jesus going to Jerusalem for the Passover?

2) Joseph and Mary searched for three days before they found Him. Why is that significant?

3) They found Him teaching in the Temple. What verse in Peter's first letter corresponds to this discovery?

4) By now, you should have discovered what event this Luke 2 narrative corresponds to in the rest of the Gospels. Compare and contrast Mary's reaction here to Mary's reaction at that other event.

5) Compare and contrast Jesus' going "down to Nazareth" to Acts 1:6-12.

6) Compare and contrast the apparent disobedience Jesus showed in staying at the Temple to His treatment before Pontius Pilate.

7) In Hebrew, the word "to hear" also means "to obey." How does this change your understanding of what it means to have the Gospel proclaimed to us in the liturgy?

8) Compare Luke 2:40 and 2:52 with 1 Sam 2:26. Given our earlier study of Samuel and David, why is it significant that these passages parallel one another?

A Guide to the Reading

This passage is located immediately after the passage which states "all the prescriptions of the law" concerning Jesus "have been fulfilled" (Luke 2:39) and immediately before the story of his public ministry. Thus, this Jesus returns to the Temple in two senses: He returns home as he had returned to his home, Nazareth, in the previous passage (Lk 2:39), and He returns to the Temple in which the Gospel itself, and the Infancy Narrative in particular, both begin (Luke 1:8-9) and end (Luke 24:53).

The passage emphasizes twin ideas, obedience and teaching ministry. Mary and Joseph lose Jesus because of apparent disobedience — He did not follow His parents in the caravan. The climax of the passage indicates, however, that He was being obedient — He was doing what his Father required. "I must be in my Father's house" (CCC 516- 518, 531-532). This particular word, *dei*, occurs 18 times in this Gospel and 22 times in Acts. It indicates a "divine compulsion, often seen in obedience to a scriptural command or prophecy."

Further, after this statement, He is asserted to have been "obedient" to Mary and Joseph. The word "obedient" is translated from the Hebrew word "to hear" or "to observe" the commandments. For the Hebrews, the one through whom God declares His word is thereby a participant in His action. This most important virtue which brought Christ to perfection, the only virtue he learned (Heb 5:8, CCC 517), is exemplified here for the first time. It is a paradox; what appears to be disobedience is obedience, much as the apparent failure of the cross would be found, instead, to be a victory.

However, this occasion is also an occasion of self-revelation. Neither angel nor human intermediary declares who He is; rather, Jesus first declares himself here — He is the son of the Father (CCC 516). This is the heart of the Gospel message. He astounds the *didaskalos*, the authoritative interpreters of Mosaic law and tradition, through His knowledge and understanding of the law. It is interesting to note that this is the only time the Temple elders are given that title in this Gospel, while Christ Himself will take on the *didaskalos* title 14 times in Luke.

The phrasing of both Luke 2:40 and 2:52 recalls that of 1 Sam 2:26, which similarly describes Samuel, a great prophet of the Old Testament. Samuel is not only a prophet called by God within the Temple (1 Sam 3:7-18) and a teacher (1 Sam 3:19), but he will anoint a hidden king in Bethlehem ("House of Bread") after a *eucharasis* sacrifice (Lev 7:15-20, 1 Sam 16:1-13), and Samuel will die after that king is greatly persecuted and faces death (1 Sam 25:1).

Similarly, the themes of self-declaration, perfect teaching, and obedience in this passage are mirrored in the account of the Passion (Luke 22:70-23:3; Luke 22:42-44). In the Holy Family's journey up to Jerusalem for the Passover, Luke prefigures Christ's journey with His apostles up to Jerusalem immediately prior to his death (Luke 19:27). Luke's care to indicate the amount of time, three days, which Mary and Joseph spent looking for their son in sorrow out in the world parallels precisely the amount of time Mary will be without Him after His crucifixion, before again discovering Him in the temple of his glorified body (Luke 9:22, 13:32, 18:33, 24:7, 24:21, 24:46). She looks for Him among relatives (the Jews) and acquaintances (the Gentiles). So, too, Mary's sorrow at their separation parallels the sorrow she will experience at the foot of the cross. While Luke does not mention Mary by name among the group of women at the Crucifixion (Luke 23:49), this narrative passage prefigures what the Apostle John records. Jesus' conversation with and questioning of the teachers, men whom He would later excoriate as "white-washed tombs" (Matthew 23:27), during this three-day period reflects the gospel which he will preach even to the dead (1 Peter 4:6). Further, Christ's growth in wisdom, physical stature, and favor, that is the perfecting of physical, emotional, spiritual, and intellectual gifts, will be mirrored and completed in the ultimate perfection of Christ's glorified, post-Resurrection body (Luke 24:36-43), the Temple He will claim to be able to destroy and build back up in three days (Matthew 26:61, Mark 14:58, John 2:21).

All of these things are prefigured here at Jerusalem's Temple (CCC 534), where the Gospel of Luke will end with the apostles praising God (Luke 24:53). It is worthwhile to note that Mary, who "kept all these things in her heart" (Luke 2:52), prefigures both the experience of the apostles who will be amazed and confused at the teachings of the *didaskalos* during His life, and the ponderings of the early Christian communities after the resurrection, who reflect upon the great mystery of Jesus among them.

The Finding in the Temple both prefigures Christ's role as teacher and broadly encapsulates the events of the Passion, Death, and Resurrection of Jesus Christ. In Jesus' obedience to his Father's will, He exemplifies the obedience which will be required of Him from Gethsemane to His death. In the three days of fruitless searching, we see the foreshadowed reactions to His death of those who loved Him. In His teaching at the Temple to the "whitewashed tombs" of the Temple elders, He prefigures both His later teaching role in the Gospel and the work he would perform in Sheol during His death. Finally, in His being found in the Temple and His advancement "in wisdom, and age and favor before God and man," we see a prefigurement of the glorified, resurrected Christ.

Questions for Application

1) Have you ever done something which others thought was wrong to do but you knew had to be done?

2) What value has meditation, the kind of meditation that Mary took up as she contemplated her Son, played in your spiritual life? Have you ever considered spending time in retreat, imitating Mary in this passage?

3) Jesus tried to teach and later grew angry at the refusal to learn shown by the Pharisees, Sadducees and scribes. When have you grown upset at a willful refusal to learn about God? Have you ever refused to learn more, for fear that you would have to change your life?

Approach to Prayer

Pray Hebrews 10:1-7.
Pause in silent meditation.
Close by praying John 1:1-4.

For Individual Reading: *St. Therese of Lisieux*

In her autobiography, *Story of a Soul*, St. Therese of Lisieux reminds us that things are not always what they seem:

"Yes, I know when I show charity to others, it is simply Jesus acting in me, and the more closely I am united to Him, the more dearly I love my Sisters. If I wish to increase this love in my heart, and the devil tries to bring before me the defects of a Sister, I hasten to look for her virtues, her good motives; I call to mind that though I may have seen her fall once, no doubt she has gained many victories over herself, which in her humility she conceals. It is even possible that what seems to me a fault, may very likely, on account of her good intention, be an act of virtue. I have no difficulty in persuading myself of this, because I have had the same experience.

"One day, during recreation, the portress came to ask for a Sister to help her. I had a childish longing to do this work, and it happened the choice fell upon me.

"I therefore began to fold up our needlework, but so slowly that my neighbour, who I knew would like to take my place, was ready before me. The Sister who had asked for help, seeing how deliberate I was, said laughingly: "I thought you would not add this pearl to your crown, you are so extremely slow," and all the Community thought I had yielded to natural reluctance.

"I cannot tell you what profit I derived from this incident, and it made me indulgent towards others. It still checks any feelings of vanity, when I am praised, for I reflect that since my small acts of virtue can be mistaken for imperfections, why should not my imperfections be mistaken for virtue? And I say with St. Paul: "To me it is a very small thing to be judged by you, or by man's day. But neither do I judge myself. He that judgeth me is the Lord"(1 Corinthians 4:3-4).

"And it is the Lord, it is Jesus, Who is my judge. Therefore I will try always to think leniently of others, that He may judge me leniently, or rather not at all, since He says: "Judge not, and ye shall not be judged"(Luke 6:37).

-From *Story of a Soul*, Chapter 9, "Night of the Soul"

Session 6: Jesus Curses the Fig Tree

Setting the Context

This session introduces the last major principle necessary to draw out the four-fold sense of Scripture. We have already seen (1) how to use matched pairs, (2) how to use the "Simon of Cyrene" principle, in which multiple items together carry the representation of a single thing and (3) how to use the meaning of place and personal names in interpretation. Now we will see the last principle: how Scripture interprets Scripture.

We will concentrate on using it as the main principle to interpret a passage. The story of Jesus cursing the fig tree occurs in both Matthew and Mark. In order to understand why Jesus cursed the fig tree, we have to understand what the fig tree represents to the Hebrews. In other words, we have to take a close look at what Scripture itself has to say about the fig tree, its leaves and its fruit.

This may well be the most difficult study in terms of the amount of Scripture work. Do a word search on "fig" and "fig tree" in Scripture using an electronic Bible or a textual concordance. Look at the context of as many occurrences as you can and consider how the fig tree is being used in each passage. In some passages, the use will be literal (e.g., leaves for clothes in Genesis 3), in others, the discussion will be more figurative (e.g., what would the fig tree have to surrender in order to gain authority over others in Judges 9? Or what does the fig signify in 1 Kings 4, Proverbs 27 or the Song of Songs?). In addition to these passages, consider Ezekiel 17:24.

Now, consider also (1) Both "Bethphage" and "Bethany" mean the "House of Figs" and (2) the Temple priests dwelt in Bethphage. Take all of what you have studied in consideration when you form your answer.

Scripture Reading

Mark 11:1-33

When they drew near to Jerusalem and Bethany at the mount of Olives, he sent two of his disciples, And said to them: "Go into the nearby village, and you shall find a colt tied, upon which no man yet has sat: loose him, and bring him. And if any man says to you, 'What are you doing?' Say, 'the Lord has need of him' and he will let him come." And going their way, they found the colt tied outside the gate, in the crossroads and they loosed him. And some of them that stood there, said to them, "What are you doing, untying the colt?"

They replied as Jesus had commanded them; and they let him go with them. And they brought the colt to Jesus; and they lay their garments on him, and he sat upon it. And many spread their garments in the path, while others cut down boughs from the trees, and strewed them in the way. And they that went before and they that followed, cried out: "Hosanna, blessed is he that comes in the name of the Lord. Blessed be the kingdom of our father David that is to come: Hosanna in the highest!"

And he entered into Jerusalem, into the temple and, having viewed all things round about, since it was now evening, he went out to Bethany with the twelve. And the next day when they came out from Bethany, he was hungry. He saw far off a fig tree with leaves, he came to see if there were any thing on it. When he came to it, he found nothing but leaves, for it was not the time for figs. And he said to it in reply: "May no man ever eat your fruit again for ever!" His disciples heard it. They came to Jerusalem, and when he entered into the temple, he began to cast out those that sold and bought in the temple, and overthrew the tables of the moneychangers, and the chairs of those that sold doves.

He did not allow any man to carry a vessel through the temple; And he taught, saying to them, "Is it not written, 'My house shall be called the house of prayer to all nations?' But you have made it a den of thieves." When the chief priests and the scribes heard, they sought how they might destroy him, for they feared him, because the whole multitude admired his doctrine. And when evening came, he went forth out of the city. And when they passed by the next morning, they saw the fig tree dried up from the roots.

And Peter remembering, said to him: "Rabbi, behold the fig tree, which you cursed is withered away!" And Jesus answering, said to them, "Have the faith of God. Amen I say to you, that whosoever shall say to this mountain, 'Be thou removed and be cast into the sea,' and shall not stagger in his heart, but believe, that whatever he said shall be done; it shall be done unto him. Therefore I say unto you, all things whatever you ask when you pray, believe that you shall receive; and they shall come to you. And when you stand to pray, forgive, if you have anything against any man; that your Father also, who is in heaven, may forgive you your sins.

But if you will not forgive, neither will your Father that is in heaven, forgive you your sins." And they came again to Jerusalem. And when he was walking in the temple, there came to him the chief priests and the scribes and the ancients, And they said to him: By what authority do you do these things? Who has given you authority to do this? And Jesus answering, said to them, "I will also ask you one word, and answer you me, and I will tell you by what authority I do these things. The baptism of John, was it from heaven, or from men? Answer me."

But they thought with themselves, saying "If we say, 'From heaven;' he will say, 'Why then did you not believe him?' If we say, 'From men,' we fear the people. For all men counted John a prophet indeed." And they answered Him, "We know not." And Jesus answering, said to them, "Neither do I tell you by what authority I do these things."

Questions for Careful Reading

1) In 1 Kings 4:25, living under the fig tree is a sign of peaceful happiness. Why might such a life be a sign of peace and happiness?

2) We saw that "Bethlehem" means "House of Bread" so that Jesus dwelling in the "House of Bread" is a sign of the Eucharist. Both "Bethphage" and "Bethany" means "House of Figs" and the high priests dwelt in the House of Figs. What does the fig tree represent if read in light of Judges 9:10-11?

3) In Genesis 3, fig leaves are used as clothes to hide Adam's shame. Seen through that lens, what might it mean to encounter a tree having nothing but leaves?

4) Find two more passages mentioning fig trees, fig leaves or the fig itself. How do each of these passage affect the interpretation of the fig tree that is out of season?

5) Construct an interpretation which explains why Jesus cursed the fig tree using the Scripture passages you have found.

A Guide to the Reading

As can be seen, the word study is extremely useful. By studying all the ways in which God uses a specific word or phrase, we build up various connotations that echo within our minds every time we see that word or phrase in the future. This is a very useful resonance to have in our heads when listening to the Sunday Gospel readings.

According to John's Gospel, Jesus had stayed in Bethany the night before His entry into Jerusalem. After the cleansing of the Temple, He returns to Bethany, the dwelling place of Lazarus, whom Jesus raised from the dead.

The words "Bethany" and "Bethphage" mean "House of Misery" or "House of Unripe Figs."

Jesus' cursing of the fig tree immediately after His stay at Bethany thus completes several Old Testament themes His Jewish followers knew quite well. The symbol of the fig tree runs throughout Scripture. Fig leaves provide Adam and Eve with clothes after the Fall (Gen 3:7), thus the leaves themselves are associated with the hiding of our shame and sin. Resting under the branches of the fig tree is a sign of eternal peace (1 Kings 4:25, Prov 27:18, John 1:48) because someone who sits beneath the fig tree has all the fruit he needs to satisfy his hunger.

However, a fig tree without fruit signifies someone who has authority over others (Judges 9:10-11). Since the high priests live in the House of Figs, the high priests' authority, rightly used, can be seen as the fruit of the law.

The fig tree Jesus encounters resonates in several ways with the Temple priests. They offer sacrifices which are meant to cover over the sins of the people. They have authority over those people, and their sacrifices are meant to bring the people of Israel into eternal peace.

But what happens to the fig tree is likewise fraught with meaning. The withering of a green tree is a sign of God's power (Ezekiel 17:24), and an army of locusts can cause the fig tree to wither (Joel 1:6-7).

Jesus knows his apostles are aware of all of these connections. So, when Jesus explains the importance of faith (verses 21-22) right after He curses the fig tree, He intends His apostles to use the faith they have been given as a unifying idea to interpret the earlier Old Testament passages they know so well.

The fig tree without fruit is a symbol of the authority of the Levitical priests. Unrighteous priests, those who misuse their authority, might well be considered an army of locusts who eat up the fruit of rightful authority.

Jesus has just cleansed the Temple. Now, He withers the fig tree and follows that act by holding a discussion with the Temple priests. According to John 17:1-2, the Father is the source of Jesus' authority, yet in this passage the chief priests and elders deny knowing the source of Jesus' authority.

Thus, if we are aware of how the fig tree is portrayed in the Old Testament, we can see that Jesus' cursing of the fig tree was actually a prophecy concerning the discussion He was about to have with the priests. The fruitless fig tree, symbol of their authority, is withered by God Himself because the priests no longer know God. They have lost faith. They cannot clothe themselves with authority any longer to hide their own shameful ignorance. In cursing the fig tree, Jesus essentially says that the Levitical priests are a marauding army of locusts who will eat up the fruit of Israel. In the Acts 2 account of Pentecost, Peter will refer to the book of Joel, and thereby draw to mind its plague of locusts, in order to make a similar point about the Romans, the "lawless men" ("lawless" because they do not know the Mosaic law) who put Jesus to death.

Questions for Application

1) When have you worked for someone who did not know how to use their authority properly?

2) When have you acted in a way that undermined or destroyed your own authority?

3) Scripture tells us to pray for those in authority. Given what you have read and discussed here, why is that important?

Approach to Prayer

Pray 1 Corinthians 9:6-10.

Pause for meditation.

Close by praying the Hail Mary.

For Individual Reading: *Padre Pio*

Padre Pio was a priest of the Capuchin order who lived in a monastic community at San Giovanni Rotondo, near Foggia, in the province of Puglia. Ordained in 1910, he embraced the life of the priest with fervent devotion. He loved the confessional, hearing confessions for up to eighteen hours a day. He would often be transported into visionary ecstasy during the consecration of the Mass, holding the Body of Christ aloft for worship for ten minutes at a time. This ecstatic love for God angered parishioners who wanted Mass to be over quickly. His desire to live a holy life was felt by many to be an insult to the way they lived their own lives.

But where sin abounds, grace abounds more. On September 20, 1918, he was graced with the divine gift of the stigmata. When a saint receives the stigmata, he bears in his hands, feet and side the wounds of Christ, painful wounds which bleed continuously. This external sign of holiness was the last straw for his enemies. They began to spread lies about him.

As a result of the false accusations, his superiors were forced to investigate his life. By June 1921, he was forbidden from saying public Mass, from receiving visitors, even from talking to women alone. Though it took ten years, he was eventually cleared of all charges. But this did not stop the falsehoods. He would be calumnied so severely during his life that he would be placed under investigation over a dozen times.

In every investigation, in every restriction, he would obey the orders of his superiors to the last detail. He never replied publicly to a single charge made against him; rather, he left it to the Church. In every case, investigation determined that the charges were false and identified those who had falsely instigated them. In several cases, the false charges had been made by cardinals, bishops and other priests. As the investigators for the cause of his beatification observed:

"Conscious of the commitments which he had undertaken when he entered the consecrated life, he observed with generosity the vows he had professed. He was obedient in all things to the commands of his Superiors, even when they were burdensome. His obedience was supernatural in intention, universal in its scope and complete in its execution. He lived the spirit of poverty with total detachment from self, from earthly goods, from his own comfort and from honours. He always had a great love for the virtue of chastity. His behaviour was modest in all situations and with all people.

"He sincerely thought of himself as useless, unworthy of God's gifts, full of weakness and infirmity, and at the same time blessed with divine favours. Amid so much admiration around him, he would say: 'I only want to be a poor friar who prays.' "

On 20 February 1971, barely three years after his death, Pope Paul VI, speaking to the Superiors of the Capuchin Order, said of him: "Look what fame he had, what a worldwide following gathered around him! But why? Perhaps because he was a philosopher? Because he was wise? Because he had resources at his disposal? Because he said Mass humbly, heard confessions from dawn to dusk and was – it is not easy to say it – one who bore the wounds of our Lord. He was a man of prayer and suffering."

His beatification drew the largest crowd in the history of the Church. Even today, when Italians were asked what institution or person they would most likely turn to when in need of help, fifty-three percent named Padre Pio.

Session 7: The Imprisonment of Peter

Setting the Context

For the last two lessons of this Scripture study, we will put into practice the various principles that we have developed over the course of the previous six. Because these passages will be drawn from Acts, every aspect of both passages will point us back toward the Paschal Mystery; that is, both passages will illuminate the Passion, Death, Resurrection and Ascension of Christ.

However, as you will see, the two passages we are about to study will accomplish this illumination in two very different ways. We will first look at how the Paschal Mystery is echoed within the physical aspects of a particular historical event. In the nesxt lesson, we will see how the apostles created the same kind of echo in the context of preaching a specific message to a specific group of people. In short, we will discover how the historical and prophetic aspects of the Old Testament are combined together in the Book of Acts.

If you find it difficult to tease out the typological meaning of this lesson's passage, read John's account of the Passion, then consider the following aspects of the passage in Acts: the time of the year Peter was arrested, what sleep may be a figure for, Peter's sleeping arrangements (verse 6), exactly how Peter was awakened by the angel, etc. When read in light what we have learned so far, the connections should become clearer.

Scripture Reading

Acts 12:1-17

At that time, Herod the king stretched forth his hands, to afflict some of the church. He killed James, the brother of John, with the sword. And seeing that it pleased the Jews, he proceeded to arrest Peter also. It was the feast of Unleavened Bread. And when he had captured him, he cast him into prison, delivering him to four squads of soldiers to be kept. He intended, after the Passover, to bring him forth to the people. Peter therefore was kept in prison. But prayer was made without ceasing by the church to God for him.

And on the same night Herod would have brought him to trial, Peter was sleeping between two soldiers, bound with two chains: and the keepers outside watched the doors of the prison. And behold an angel of the Lord stood by him: and a light shone in the room. The angel struck Peter on the side, raised him up and said, "Arise quickly." And the chains fell off from his hands. The angel said to him, "Gird yourself, and put on your sandals." He did so. The angel added, "Cast your garment about yourself, and follow me." And going out, Peter followed him. He did not know this was really happening, he thought he saw a vision. And passing through the first and the second guards, they came to the iron gate that leads to the city. The gate opened itself for them. And going out, they passed on through a street: and immediately the angel departed from him.

Peter realized what had happened and said, "Now I know the Lord has indeed sent his angel, and has delivered me out of the hand of Herod, and from all the expectation of the people of the Jews."

As he contemplated this, he came to the house of Mary the mother of John, who was surnamed Mark, where many were gathered together and praying. When he knocked at the door of the gate, a damsel named Rhoda heard him. When she heard Peter's voice, she was so happy, she did not open the gate but instead ran in and told the others that Peter stood at the gate. But they said to her, "You are mad." But she insisted it was so. Then said they, "It is his angel." But Peter continued knocking. When they opened, they saw him, and were astonished. But he beckoned to them with his hand to hold their peace and told how the Lord had brought him out of prison, and he said "Tell these things to James, and to the brethren." And going out, he went to another place.

Now when day came, there was no small stir among the soldiers, concerning what was become of Peter. When Herod sought for him and found him not, he examined the keepers and commanded they should be put to death. Then he went down from Judea to Caesarea, and lived there.

Herod was angry with the Tyrians and the Sidonians. But they with one accord came to him, and having won over Blastus, the king's chamberlain, they asked for peace, because their countries were nourished by him. Upon a day appointed, Herod being arrayed in kingly apparel, sat in the judgment seat, and spoke to the people. And the people cried out, "It is the voice of a god, and not of a man." And immediately an angel of the Lord struck him, because he had not given the honour to God. He was eaten up by worms and died. But the word of the Lord increased and multiplied. And Barnabas and Saul returned from Jerusalem, having fulfilled their ministry, taking with them John, who was surnamed Mark.

Questions for Careful Reading

Today, there is but a single task.

List as many correspondences as you can between the events here and the events in the Passion narratives as they are described in the four Gospels. How many did you find?

A Guide to the Reading

New Testament passages referenced:
v. 12:1-2 — Mt 14:10

John the Baptist is beheaded before Jesus' arrest; James is killed by the sword before Peter's arrest. These are the only two people killed by the sword in the New Testament.

v. 12:3 — Mark 14:1

Jesus' arrest took place during the week of Unleavened Bread; so does Peter's.

v. 12:4 — John 19:23

The Cross was guarded by four soldiers; Peter was guarded by four squads of four soldiers.

v. 12:5 — Luke 22:1

In all of Scripture, only Peter is recorded as having the whole Church praying for him.

v. 12:6 — Mt 27:38, Mark 15:27, Luke 23:32, John 19:18, Mat 27:45

Jesus hung in darkness for three hours between two thieves; Peter sleeps in darkness between two soldiers.

v. 12:7 — John 19:34

As Jesus slept in death, a soldier pierced his side with a lance; as Peter sleeps in prison, an angel kicks him in the side.

v. 12:8 — Mt 27:28

Jesus was stripped of his clothes before the crucifixion; Peter apparently was also stripped of his, for he had to wrap a mantle around himself before he could leave with the angel. Peter clothes himself in his mantle before he leaves the prison; Jesus clothes himself in His resurrected body before He leaves the tomb.

v. 12:10 — Luke 24:46, 1 Peter 3:19
   Jesus passed three days in the prison of death; Peter passes through three checkpoints as he leaves prison. We pass through three sacraments of initiation into the Church (Baptism, Confirmation and Eucharist) – Baptism is specifically linked to Jesus' death (Romans 6:1-4).

v. 12:12 — John 19:26-27
   Jesus gives John to His mother, Mary, while Peter first turns to the house of Mary, mother of (a different) John.

v. 12:14-16 — Luke 24:4-11
   The risen Jesus is first met by women, and Peter is first met by a woman. The women in the garden met two angels,;Rhoda is accused of having seen Peter's angel. When both sets of women report what they know to the others, both reports are called nonsense. Both groups are amazed when they find the reports are true.

v. 12:17 — Acts 1:10-12
   After exiting the prison of death, Jesus ascended into heaven; after exiting the Roman prison Peter "departed and went to another place." After the Ascension, Jesus will not be seen again except in Acts 9, when He guides Paul into the Church. After Acts 12, Peter will not be seen again, except for Acts 15, when he guides the council. Similarly, one could note that after the Ascension, the Holy Spirit descended upon Peter so he might know what to say to the 3,000, while after the release from prison, Peter guides James, so James might know what to say to the council. In short, after Jesus' Ascension in Acts 1, the Holy Spirit appears in order to guide the apostles in Acts 2. After Peter "goes to another place" in Acts 10, Peter reappears in order to guide James and the council in Acts 15.

v. 12:18-19 — Mt 28:11-15

Both groups of soldiers were very concerned by what happened. The soldiers at Jesus' tomb were told to say they fell asleep, an offense which could be punished by death. The sleeping soldiers guarding Peter are punished by death. The closing scene involving Herod and the crowd reminds us of the opening scene of Christ's Passion, when Pontius Pilate presided over the crowd. Pilate avoided punishment by washing his hands of the crowd's decision, but Herod did not distance himself from the crowd's pleasure, and suffered the penalty.

v. 12:25 – John 21:24

At the end of the Gospel of John, John testifies to the truth of what he has seen. After Peter is released from prison, Barnabas and Saul bring John with them, presumably to have him testify to the rest of the Church about what he has seen.

Questions for Application

1) When have you had a very bad experience that turned out to be the necessary prelude to a wonderful experience?

2) Conversely, have you ever been rescued from a terrible situation, a situation that you could not escape on your own? How did your experience correspond to Peter's?

3) Do you know anyone who has suffered severe persecution? How has their attitude been like or unlike Peter's?

Approach to Prayer

Pray 1 Corinthians 10:1-11.
Pause for meditation.
Close by praying together 2 Corinthians 3:12-16.

For Individual Reading: *St. John Bosco*

In the last chapter of his autobiography, *Memoirs of the Oratory*, Don Bosco relates his experience with a visitor who saved his life on more than one occasion:

"The grey dog was the topic of many conversations and various conjectures. Many of you have seen him and even petted him. Now, laying aside the fantastic stories which are told of this dog, I will tell you plainly only what is pure truth.

"The frequent attacks which had been made against me made it inadvisable for me to walk to or from the city of Turin alone. In those days, the asylum was the last building on the way to the Oratory. The rest of the way was land covered with hawthorn and acacia trees.

"One dark evening, rather late, I was making my way home with some trepidation when a huge dog appeared beside me, which at first sight gave me a start. But he seemed friendly and even nuzzled me as if I were his master. We quickly became friends, and he accompanied me as far as the Oratory. Many other times that evening's experience was repeated. Indeed, I may say that Grigio did me valuable service. Here are a few examples.

"On a wet, foggy night at the end of November 1854, I was coming from the city. So as not to have a long way to go alone, I took the street connecting Our Lady of Consolation and the Cottolengo. At one point along the street I noticed two men walking a little in front of me. They matched their pace to mine, quickening or slowing down as I did. When I crossed the road to dodge them, they crossed right over in front of me. I attempted to turn back but was not in time. For they suddenly jumped me from behind, keeping an ominous silence, and threw a cloak over my head. I fought to keep from getting tangled up but it was no use. Then one also tried to stuff a rag into my mouth. I was trying to shout but could no longer do so. At that moment Grigio appeared, and growling like a bear he leapt into the face of one man while snapping viciously at the other. They plainly would have to tangle with the dog before finishing with me.

'Call off your dog,' they began to cry, trembling with fear.

'I'll call him off,' I said, 'when you agree to leave passers-by alone.'

'Call him off quick,' they exclaimed.

"Grigio continued growling like an enraged wolf or bear. The two men took to their heels, and Grigio stayed by my side, accompanying me until I went into the Cottolengo Institute. After recovering from my scare, and refreshed by a drink which that charitable institute always seems to come up with at the right moment, I went on home with a good escort.

"Every evening when I had no other company, as I passed the [last] buildings I would see Grigio bound out of nowhere along the way. Many times the Oratory boys saw him. Once he was the centre of an amusing incident. The boys saw him coming into the courtyard. Some wanted to strike him, and others wanted to throw stones at him.

'Don't tease him,' Joseph Buzzetti ordered. 'That's Don Bosco's dog.' They turned to patting and stroking him then as they brought him along to me. I was in the refectory having supper with some seminarians and priests and with my mother. They were alarmed at the unexpected sight of the dog.

'There's no need to be afraid,' I said. 'It's my Grigio. Let him come in.'

"In fact he made a wide tour round the table and came joyfully up to me. I patted him too and offered him soup, bread, and meat, but he refused all of it. He would not even sniff at what I offered.

'Well, what do you want?' I asked. He only cocked his ears and wagged his tail.

'Either eat or drink or otherwise entertain me,' I concluded. He continued to evidence contentment, resting his head on my napkin as if he wanted to speak to me and tell me 'Good night.' Then the boys, wondering a great deal and quite happy, led him outside. I remember that I had come home late, and a friend had brought me in his carriage.

"The last time that I saw Grigio was in 1866 while I was going from Murialdo to Moticucco to see my friend Louis Muglia. The parish priest of Buttigliera wanted to accompany me part of the way and as a consequence I was surprised by nightfall only halfway on my journey.

'Oh, if only I had my Grigio,' I thought to myself, 'how fortunate I would be!' Having said that, I started across a field to take advantage of the last rays of light. Just then Grigio came bounding up to me, full of affection. He accompanied me for the stretch of road that I still had to travel, which was two miles.

"When I got to my friend's house, where I was expected, they asked me to go round another way, fearing there would be a fight between my Grigio and the family's two mastiffs. 'If they got into a fight,' said Moglia, 'they would tear each other to pieces.'

"I talked a lot with the whole family before we sat down to supper. My companion was left to rest in a corner of the room. When we had finished our meal, my friend said, 'We must also give Grigio his supper.'

"He took a little food to bring to the dog; he looked in every corner of the room and of the house, but Grigio was not to be found. We all wondered, since neither door nor window was open, nor had the family dogs given any sign of his departure. We renewed our search upstairs, but no one could find him.

"That is the last news I had of the grey dog that was the subject of so much enquiry and discussion. I never was able to find out who was his owner, I only know that the animal was truly providential for me on many occasions when I found myself in danger."

"In answer to a query in 1870, Don Bosco remarked, 'It sounds ridiculous to call him an angel, yet he is no ordinary dog.' Don Bosco's biographers tell of several other incidents in which Grigio saved Don Bosco from assailants or kept him company on lonely walks in the dark. This 1866 appearance was the last as of the time when Don Bosco was writing his memoirs. In 1883, however, he saw the mysterious dog again while returning to Vallecrosia from Ventimiglia late one evening. He spoke of this appearance several times in different places. One of those who heard him tell the story was his French biographer Doctor Charles D'Espiney; another was Father Secondo Gay, pastor of Saint Silvester's Church in Asti, who testified to it on October 17, 1908, during the gathering of evidence for Don Bosco's beatification.

"In 1883, Don Bosco was visiting the Olive family, generous benefactors from Marseilles. He told them how he had recently met his old and faithful gray friend on the road from Ventimiglia. The astonished lady of the house observed that Grigio would have to be two or three times older than dogs normally live. Don Bosco smiled mischievously. 'Then it must have been Grigio's son or grandson,' he suggested, evading the issue she was driving at. The Salesian Sisters also claim to have experienced Grigio's protection on three occasions between 1893 and 1930."

Session 8: Peter at Pentecost

Setting the Context

In this passage, Peter is the first to demonstrate a habit that is found throughout Acts. Whenever the apostles are questioned, they respond with a couple of verses from the Old Testament and their listeners are either immediately converted or confounded. What is in those verses that causes such a shocked and shocking response?

Though Peter quotes from several Old Testament passages in Acts 2, we will look at the first alone: the quote Peter uses from the book of Joel. Different translations of Joel divide the book up differently – in some translations, Joel is divided into five chapters; in others, three chapters. For the three-chapter version, the passages he quotes are found in Joel 1:2 and 2:28-32.

To see why these passages from Joel convert 3,000 people, realize that Peter begins quoting Joel in the very first sentence he utters, "Hear, O men of Judea and all who live in Jerusalem..." That is, he is creating an ellipsis. By immediately following his Joel 1:2 reference with Joel 2:28-32, he intends his Jewish audience to recall everything that lies between those two sets of verses.

Thus, we need to do a typological analysis of the following elements of Joel 1 and 2, i.e. of the Joel passages Peter framed for his audience, in order to see why the audience reacted as it did.

This is the most difficult passage to read because we have to consider the historical situation Israel was in at the time Peter was

vv. 17-21 — Is 2:2, Joel 2:28-32

Roman soldiers were undoubtedly wandering amongst the crowd at the very moment Peter began addressing them. Peter has to communicate the Kingdom of God to his fellow Jews, who have gathered from all nations, without being himself crucified for inciting the crowd with treasonous talk. By inspiring the 120 disciples to speak of "the mighty works of God" (Acts 2:11), the Holy Spirit has already begun priming the crowd to hear the Passover proclamation Peter begins to deliver, for the disciples' review of salvation history provides the proper context for what his audience is about to hear. Through the voices of the 120, God reminds His People of the way He has always fulfilled His promises to them. Now, out of this chorus of voices, Peter's voice rises like a soloist in a symphony orchestra.

When Peter's Jewish audience hears his reference to the outpouring of the Spirit prophesied in the book of Joel, they catch his meaning immediately. By claiming the Pentecost event is prophesied in Joel, he implicitly asserts that an army of locusts has invaded the land of Israel; i.e., Joel's prophesy foreshadowed the Roman invasion of the land of Israel. Peter is calling the Romans locusts, who eat all the good things of the Promised Land through their rapacious taxation. Certainly the Jews in the audience agree with the characterization, but they certainly also have a problem with Peter's interpretation. They know the sequence of events in the book of Joel. In speaking of the outpouring of the Spirit, Peter is speaking of element three. By that reference, he thereby implicitly calls the Romans locusts, which is element one. Sadly, he seems to have forgotten about element two: the restoration. The outpouring of the Spirit cannot happen until the treasures of Israel are restored. Roman soldiers are walking through the crowd right now, and taxation certainly hasn't stopped. Clearly, the promised restoration has not yet occurred. Is Peter crazy, or just stupid? Maybe he's drunk, like his friends.

But immediately after reciting Joel's prophecy about the outpouring of the Spirit, Peter apparently changes his audience: now he speaks to all the men of Israel, that is, every man of any nation who is a Jew, a son of Israel. Peter points out that Jesus did mighty works and deeds — something no one in the crowd can deny. Jesus is, in other words, a treasure of Israel. Throughout history, God's prophets describe His plans, and Jesus was killed according to the plan of God. Peter accuses the crowd of having killed Him by the "hands of lawless men," that is, by the hands of the Romans, who were lawless because they did not possess the Law given to Israel by God on Mount Sinai. In short, Peter says that when Joel spoke of the wine, bread, and oil Temple sacrifices being consumed, he was actually speaking symbolically about Jesus. Peter is accusing the Jews of being in league with the locusts; in fact, he accuses them of being locusts themselves for having instigated the destruction of the treasure of Israel.

The crowd is, at this point, undoubtedly not very pleased with Peter. "Yes, this Jesus did great things," they might be thinking, "what of it? He's dead. Quit whining about your late, great leader."

But Peter knows something the crowd does not yet know, and he hastens to give them the information they do not have. This Jesus, the sacrifice prophesied by Joel, has been raised up. He has been, in a word, restored. One can only imagine the effect this announcement has on the crowd — dead silence? a murmur of shock, amazement? We don't know for sure. All we know for sure is that Peter is just getting warmed up.

vv. 25-28 — Ps 16:8-11

He immediately launches into a second Scripture commentary meant to support the interpretation he has just given of Joel. Peter is making the case that Joel's prophecy refers to Jesus. He goes to Psalm 16 for further support. Out of deference to the Roman soldiers wandering about, soldiers who get quite touchy when anyone talks about Jewish kingship, Peter calls David "patriarch," but every Israelite knew David as the greatest king Israel ever had. Peter pointedly calls Jesus a descendant of David, and even speaks of David's throne as the Roman soldiers stand nearby — great boldness from a man who had been cowering in a locked room just seven weeks before. With this Scripture reference, he intends his audience to remember that this Psalm speaks of the goodly heritage which comes only from the Lord, while at the same time reminding them of the history of idolatry which Israel has long had.

v. 30 — Ps 132:11, 2 Sam 7:12

By making an implicit reference to God's promise to David, Peter does two things. First, he asserts Jesus to be greater than David; second, he reminds them of the promise of Psalm 132: God would remain with Israel forever. This Psalm naturally leads his Jewish audience to also remember 2 Samuel, in which the prophetic oath forms the basis for the building of the Temple which Psalm 132 talks about. The oath in 2 Samuel is immediately preceded by the story of Michal, daughter of Saul, who was left barren because she despised the joy David took in recovering the presence of God from the pagans who had captured it (2 Sam 6:20-23). In other words, Peter is telling the Israelites that they stand on the cusp of being treated either as Michal was in 2 Samuel or as David describes in Psalm 132. Peter treats the Michal-David-Temple story as a prophecy being fulfilled before their eyes, with Jesus as David, fulfilling in His own body the construction of the Temple.

v. 31 — Ps. 16:10

Peter returns to this Psalm a second time to tie together what he has just explained. Jesus is the Christ, the Christ is resurrected, and both Joel and David prophesied every detail of what the crowd is now living out. God's plans work, and this is the culmination of God's saving plan. He is driving home the point with extraordinary power.

vv. 34-35 — Ps 110:1

Peter now has established the Scriptural basis to support the assertion he had hinted at earlier. Jesus' resurrection is the promised restoration spoken of in Joel. He finishes by reminding the crowd of the last and greatest debate Jesus had with the Pharisees, Sadducees, and scribes (Mt 22:44-46, Mk 12:35-37, Lk 20:41-44). In this debate, Jesus asked them to interpret the verse Peter now quotes. Jesus' opponents were unable to answer, but Peter knows the answer.

His Jewish audience now clearly sees that the Psalms and Joel spoke about Jesus. Joel's prophecy is about Jesus. They know the order of events in Joel: invasion, restoration, pouring out of the Spirit, and... hey, wait a minute!

If this is the pouring out of the Spirit Joel promised, then Peter was right to begin his speech by speaking to the men of Judea and Jerusalem, for this is how the final portion of Joel begins: This last address to Judea and Jerusalem in Joel begins the judgment of whole nations, of all who have stood against Israel. The phrasing in Joel is apocalyptic: God speaks of turning plowshares into swords and pruning hooks into spears, reversing the prophecies of Isaiah and Micah (Is 2:4, Mic 4:3). The weak become warriors and entire nations are crushed like grapes in a winepress. If Peter is right — and he has just demonstrated from Scripture that he is right — then each of the first three parts of the prophecy of Joel has been fulfilled. The listening crowd assembled from all the nations of the civilized world — assembled just as Joel prophesied they would be — this crowd suddenly realizes what Peter is driving at: Only the fourth part of the prophecy remains to be fulfilled, and the fourth part of the prophecy is... JUDGMENT.

They stand in the valley of judgment and they know it. This is how Peter converts 3,000 people in under three minutes. He demonstrates prophecy fulfilled, a fulfillment so vivid, so immediate, that 3,000 turn and, with one voice, ask how to be saved.

Questions for Application

1) When have you faced judgment? Was there anyone to save you?

2) Consider the situation in the world today. What events have made the larger world aware of the possibility of judgment? How has it responded?

3) Could a speech as powerful as Peter's be given today to Christians or anyone else? If so, what elements would it need to have a similar driving power?

Approach to Prayer

Pray James 5:1-6.
Pause for meditation.
Conclude by praying together Luke 5:4-10.

For Individual Reading: *G. K. Chesterton*

People have fallen into a foolish habit of speaking of orthodoxy as something heavy, humdrum, and safe. There never was anything so perilous or so exciting as orthodoxy. It was sanity: and to be sane is more dramatic than to be mad.... The orthodox Church never took the tame course or accepted the conventions; the orthodox Church was never respectable.... It is easy to be a madman: it is easy to be a heretic. It is always easy to let the age have its head; the difficult thing is to keep one's own. It is always easy to be a modernist; as it is easy to be a snob.... It is always simple to fall; there are an infinity of angles at which one falls, only one at which one stands. To have fallen into any one of the fads from Gnosticism to Christian Science would indeed have been obvious and tame. But to avoid them all has been one whirling adventure; and in my vision the heavenly chariot flies thundering through the ages, the dull heresies sprawling and prostrate, the wild truth reeling but erect.

- *Orthodoxy*, (Garden City, NY: Doubleday, 1908, p. 100)

Recommended Bibles

Despite the enormous number of Bibles available in the English language, Catholics have only a small set that are approved for use in Bible studies.

If you can read Latin, the Latin Vulgate (written 390-405 AD) was the Catholic standard for nearly two millennia. Sadly, most Latin-rite Catholics don't understand Latin.

From roughly the time of the Council of Trent, the Douay-Rheims Version (1582-1610) was the standard for English speakers. Unfortunately, the 1610 edition uses language which is extremely archaic by modern standards. Fortunately, many of the most difficult passages were updated by Bishop Challoner between 1749 and 1777, thus producing the Challoner-Rheims Version. Unfortunately, it's been over two centuries since that update, and even the Challoner version is no longer as readable as it once was.

The Confraternity Version of the New Testament, published in 1941, was meant to update Challoner's translation, but as the name implies, only the New Testament was actually completed. The Old Testament was not similarly updated. In the same way, the generally excellent 1955 Knox Translation only has the New Testament approved for use.

The Revised Standard Version, Catholic Edition (1965), the original Jerusalem Bible (1966), and the original New American Bible (pre-1970) are all acceptable for study. Unfortunately, serious students of Scripture are forced to avoid the New Jerusalem Bible and the post-1970 versions of the New American Bible, since those translations employ gender-neutral language. This absolutely atrocious style of translation removes most masculine pronouns and references, e.g., where the text says "man" the translators replace it with "human". As a result, the prophetic passages of the Old Testament concerning Christ are removed; the butchered translation essentially destroys the ability to fully utilize the four-fold sense in the interpretation of Scripture. To make matters worse, the revised NAB (post-1970 versions) has footnotes which are quite misleading in many instances; in some cases the sense of the footnotes is simply erroneous.

While it is true that the version of Scripture used in the liturgy is the New American Bible (NAB), it is a version of the NAB which Rome has corrected so as to avoid the gender-neutral language and the more egregious examples of poor translation. Unfortunately, it is not possible to purchase a version of the NAB that matches what we hear in the liturgy.

So, what version of the Scriptures is recommended for study? Unfortunately, the only English Scripture translation which is both modern and complete, and which has not been mutilated by the rapidly aging crowd of politically correct "Scripture scholars", is the Revised Standard Version, Catholic edition (RSV-CE). It would be pleasant if Catholics had a wider choice, but we do not.

Recommended Further Reading

Bible Basics

This extremely thorough explanation of the Faith provides numerous examples of how to use the four senses of Scripture in apologetics, the Scriptural defense of the Faith.

The Flesh of God: A Six-Week Study of the Infancy Narratives

This Scripture study uses a different format to demonstrate the use of the four senses in the first two chapters of Matthew and Luke, the infancy narratives.

Artfully Teaching the Faith

This slim volume shows how medieval and Renaissance artists visually embedded Catholic doctrine within the symbols used in their artwork; that is, it provides visual examples of how the greatest artists in history used the four senses in their work.

Effective Habits of the Five People You Meet in Heaven

This study of the modern novel, *The Five People You Meet in Heaven*, shows that the four senses apply not only to Scripture, but even to modern literary works. Specifically, it demonstrates how Mitch Albom's best-selling novel is actually an allegory of Catholic Faith, a superb explanation of Purgatory and what it means to lead a virtuous life.

Sex and the Sacred City

Demonstrates how our very bodies are actually able to represent the four senses of divine meaning. It summarizes Pope John Paul II's synthesis of Christian theology, the Theology of the Body.

Want to learn more but don't have time to read?

Consider

Bridegroom Press Audio Selections

- *Harmonizing Science and Religion*

- *I Was A Pro-Life Atheist*

- *Effectively Teaching the Faith*

- *Four Questions in Church History:*
  Crusades, Inquisition, Galileo, and the Holocaust

- *The Crime of Galileo*

- *The Inquisition*

- *Effective Habits of the Five People*
  You Meet in Heaven

- *Fact and Fiction in the Da Vinci Code*

CDs and MP3s for your sound system
www.bridegroompress.com

Printed in the United Kingdom
by Lightning Source UK Ltd.
122841UK00001B/257/A